Let's COOK!

Written by Pamela Gwyther
Photography by Mark Wood

BACKPACKBOOKS

·

NEW YORK

Please note:
Recipes using raw or very lightly cooked eggs should be avoided
by infants, the elderly, pregnant women, convalescents, and anyone
suffering from an illness.

This 2008 edition published by Backpack Books,
by arrangement with Parragon.

With special thanks to our models Sophie Collins, Zion Duharty,
Fran Eames and Kristal Lau

Home economist: Pamela Gwyther

ISBN-13: 978-0-7607-9483-8
ISBN-10: 0-7607-9483-9

Printed and bound in China

10 9 8 7 6 5 4 3 2 1

CONTENTS

THE MAGIC OF COOKING

Everyone enjoys eating delicious food, but cooking it can be even more fun. Cooking is a kind of magic. In a couple of hours you can change a piece of raw dough into a tray of warm, mouth-watering bread rolls!

To be a good cook, you need to get everything ready in the kitchen before you start. Follow the recipe steps carefully, and make sure you use your cooking equipment in the right way. Take a few minutes to read these pages, and then you'll be ready to GET COOKING!

You will find these symbols on your recipe pages:

| serves 2 | makes 6 | preparation time | cooking time | no cooking needed | chilling time | freezing time |

WEIGHING AND MEASURING

- A recipe will work much better if you weigh or measure your ingredients accurately. Guessing is not a good idea!

- Use measuring cups and spoons for dry ingredients such as flour and sugar. All the recipes use standard level cup, tablespoon, and teaspoon measures.

- Use a measuring jug for liquids—make sure you place the jug on a flat surface.

SAFETY FIRST!

- Look out for the  ⚠ symbol in the recipes. When you see this ask for adult help to:

  – move food in and out of a hot oven,
  – cook on the hob,
  – use a sharp knife,
  – use an electrical appliance such as a blender or a food processor.

- Always wear oven mitts when handling hot dishes, pans, and trays.

- Remember to switch off your oven when you have finished cooking.

- When cooking on a hob, turn the pan handle to one side to avoid the heat. This also makes it harder to knock the pan off accidentally.

- Hold a pan handle steady with one hand while you stir.

- Always put hot pans on a heatproof mat when you remove them from the hob.

- Always chop or cut food on a chopping board, not on your work surface.

- Keep sharp knives in a knife block or a safety wrapper when not in use.

- Never walk around with a sharp knife in your hand.

- Make sure your hands are dry when plugging and unplugging electrical equipment.

- Wipe up any spills on the floor straight away.

CLEAN AND TIDY

- Always wash your hands before you start to cook. When making pastry or bread, scrub your nails clean.

- Roll up your sleeves and always wear an apron.

- Tie back your hair if it's long.

- Make sure work surfaces and equipment are clean.

- Use clean dish towels. Use a different towel to dry your hands.

- Wash your chopping board and knife in between different uses, especially after cutting up raw meat.

COOKING TIPS

Read through the recipe and make sure you have bought all the necessary ingredients. Some recipes are more difficult than others and need lots of ingredients. All the recipes in this book are graded as ★ easy ★★ medium ★★★ difficult (you may need adult help for these)

Check through the equipment list for each recipe before you start.

Here are a few useful tips about some of the basic cooking skills that you will use for the recipes in this book.

WHISKING

You whisk air into egg whites or cream to make them lighter. An electric hand mixer is a help, but a balloon whisk will also do the job.

FOLDING IN

Using a metal spoon or a plastic spatula, carefully fold one mixture into another until all the ingredients are mixed together.

RUBBING IN

When making pastry or biscuits, you rub the butter and flour between your fingertips until the mixture looks like breadcrumbs.

ROLLING OUT

When rolling out pastry, lightly flour the surface and the rolling pin. Roll out the pastry dough gently, without stretching it.

SEPARATING EGGS

Crack the shell and pour the egg onto a saucer. Place an eggcup over the yolk and pour the white into a bowl. Use the yolk as needed.

LINING A PAN

Line the pan with baking parchment when making brownies or flapjacks. It stops the cakes sticking to the pan.

MELTING

When melting chocolate, make sure the bottom of the bowl doesn't touch the water in the pan. If the chocolate gets too hot, it will be spoiled!

KNEADING

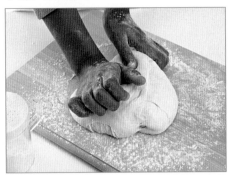

You knead bread dough to make it stretchy so it will hold in air when cooking. Pull and stretch the dough with your hands until smooth.

SUPER SNACKS

Wraps, rolls, and snacks—here's lots of easy-to-eat food for when you want a quick snack or something tasty to nibble. There are delicious ideas for all kinds of occasions, from a sleepover party to filling your lunch box.

Try vegetable sticks and dips, tortillas or tarts—and there's even a recipe for home-made bread. To go with your super snacks, whip up a fruit and yogurt smoothie in seconds to make a power-packed drink.

serves 8

30 minutes

no cooking

STICKS AND DIPS

Crudités are fab finger food—great for lunch boxes, parties or just when you have the munchies! Chunky sticks of raw vegetables with dreamy flavored dips—m'mmmm!

Equipment

- chopping board
- sharp knife
- mixing bowl
- wooden spoon
- measuring cups and spoons
- food processor
- serving plate
- 2 small bowls
- measuring jug

What you need:

Crudités

4 carrots, peeled

2 zucchini

4 stalks of celery

half a cucumber

1 red bell pepper

1 yellow bell pepper

8 baby corns

Cheesy Dip

1 cup cream cheese

2 tbsp milk

2 scallions, finely chopped

1 tbsp freshly chopped parsley

1 tbsp chives

salt and freshly ground black pepper

Hummus

14 oz canned chickpeas, drained

juice of 1 lemon

2 cloves of garlic, crushed

2 tbsp tahini (sesame paste)

½ cup olive oil

salt and freshly ground black pepper

freshly chopped parsley and paprika to garnish

CRUDITÉS and CHEESY DIP

1. Cut the carrots, zucchini, and celery into sticks 2½ inches long. Halve the cucumber, remove the seeds, and cut into equal-sized sticks.

2. Halve the peppers and remove the seeds. Cut each half into long strips.

3. Make the cheesy dip by mixing the cheese and milk until smooth. Add the other ingredients and season.

HUMMUS

4. Blend the chickpeas, lemon juice, and garlic in the processor. Add the tahini and blend until smooth.

5. Keep the machine running and add the oil, a little at a time. Season.

6. Put the dip and hummus in small bowls. Sprinkle hummus with parsley and paprika. Put the bowls on a serving plate with the crudités around them.

FUNKY FRUIT SMOOTHIES ★

serves 4

5 minutes

no cooking

Check out these delicious fruit smoothies, which you can mix up in minutes. Simply choose any of your favorite fruits and get creative with different mixtures to make some really zany drinks!

Equipment

- chopping board
- sharp knife
- blender or food processor
- measuring jug
- measuring cups and spoons

What you need:

Berry Smoothie

1 small banana

6 oz fresh raspberries and strawberries

1 1/4 cups milk

superfine sugar if required

Yogurt Smoothie

1 small banana

1 ripe pear

3/4 cup apple juice

3/4 cup natural yogurt

1 tsp vanilla extract

1 tbsp runny honey

BERRY SMOOTHIE

1. For the berry smoothie, slice the banana. Halve the strawberries if they are very large.

2. Place the fruit in the blender. Pour in the milk. Make sure the lid is on tight and blend until smooth.

3. Taste and add sugar if required. Pour into smoothie glasses and serve with straws.

YOGURT SMOOTHIE

1. For the yogurt smoothie, slice the banana. Peel, core, and chop the pear.

2. Place all the ingredients in the blender. Make sure the lid is on tight and blend until smooth.

3. Pour into smoothie glasses and serve.

For a change!
You can add crushed ice or ice cream to your smoothie to make a cooler drink for hot summer days.

makes 4

10–15 minutes

10 minutes

PACK-A-PITA

This recipe is easy and great fun! You can use pita breads to make some really crazy snacks, adding almost anything you like as a filling.

Equipment

- chopping board
- sharp knife
- mixing bowl
- fork
- wooden spoon
- small pan
- slotted spoon
- measuring cups and spoons
- plastic wrap or foil

What you need:

2 large pita breads

Filling

½ cup canned tuna, drained

2 scallions

½ cup canned corn, drained

2 tbsp mayonnaise

salt and freshly ground black pepper

2 eggs

2 little romaine lettuces

For a change!

Mix cold cooked chicken with mayonnaise and shredded lettuce. Spice up your mayonnaise by adding a little curry powder and a teaspoon of apricot jam.

For a veggie pita, use cream cheese mixed with chopped chives, baby spinach leaves, and cherry tomatoes cut in half.

1. Warm the pita breads under the broiler or in the oven. Cut each pita in half to make two pouches.

2. In a mixing bowl, flake the tuna with a fork. Finely chop the scallions and add to the bowl.

3. Add the corn and mayonnaise and mix together. Season well.

14

4. Boil the eggs in a small pan for 10 minutes. Cool under cold running water. Peel and roughly chop the eggs and add to the mix.

5. Wash and slice the lettuce. Place inside each pita pouch.

6. Spoon in the savory filling. Eat now or wrap in plastic wrap or foil until needed.

CRUNCHY JACKETS

For a cozy evening at home, hot jacket potatoes are a brilliant meal. You can stuff them with your favorite fillings and eat them piping hot from the oven!

What you need:

4 large potatoes, about 8 oz each

½ stick or ¼ cup butter

salt and freshly ground black pepper

½ cup ham

1 cup grated Cheddar cheese

For a change!

For a veggie option try some fried mushrooms instead of the ham.

Add flaked canned tuna or salmon to the mashed potato instead of ham.

For an extra tasty meal, halve the hot potatoes and pour over some chili sauce or bolognese sauce. Sprinkle with cheese to finish.

1. Preheat the oven to 400°F. Wash and wipe the potatoes. Prick with a fork and place on a baking sheet.

2. Cook the potatoes in the oven for 60–75 minutes until they are soft inside and the skins are crisp. Remove them from the oven.

3. Cut each potato in half and scoop out the soft insides into the mixing bowl. Take care not to damage the skins.

4. Mash the potato well with the fork. Add the butter and season.

5. Place the skins on the baking sheet. Chop the ham and put some into each shell. Spoon in the potato.

6. Sprinkle the grated cheese on the potatoes. Put them back in the oven and cook for a further 15 minutes until the tops are golden.

serves 4

15 minutes +
1 hour marinating

5–6 minutes

Equipment

- sharp knife
- chopping board
- nonmetallic dish
- measuring spoons
- wooden spoon
- plastic wrap
- bowl
- fork
- skillet
- slotted spoon
- large serving plate
- 2 small bowls

FAJITAS ARE FUN!

Fajitas taste sensational! They come from Mexico and are soft tortillas filled with meat, salad, and some spicy sauce. You'll have a fab time making them!

What you need:

1 red and 1 yellow bell pepper

2 skinless chicken breast fillets

2 tbsp olive oil

2 tsp mild chili powder

1 tsp paprika

juice and grated rind of 1 lime

salt and freshly ground black pepper

4 soft flour tortillas

1–2 handfuls shredded iceberg lettuce

4 tbsp sour cream or plain yogurt

Spicy Tomato and Avocado Sauce

2 tomatoes, seeded and chopped

1 small red onion, very finely chopped

1 tbsp lime juice

1 tbsp olive oil

1 avocado, peeled, pitted, and diced

1 tbsp chopped fresh cilantro

1. Halve the peppers, remove the seeds, and cut into long strips. Cut the chicken fillets into strips and place in a nonmetallic dish.

2. Add half the oil, the spices, lime juice and rind. Season. Mix until the chicken is well coated. Cover and leave in the fridge for 1 hour.

3. To make the spicy tomato sauce, mix together all the ingredients. Season, cover, and keep cool.

4. Heat the remaining oil in a skillet. Fry the chicken, stirring, for 3 minutes. Add the peppers and fry for 3 minutes, until the chicken is cooked.

5. Remove pan from heat. Spoon out the chicken and peppers and keep warm. Heat the tortillas in the oven. Put the sauce and cream in bowls.

6. To make your fajita, put some sauce and sour cream onto a tortilla. Add the chicken, peppers, and lettuce. Roll up your fajita and eat it!

For a change!

Use cooked ground beef instead of chicken.

For a veggie option, use grated cheese instead of chicken or beef.

makes 8

15 minutes
+ 1 hour marinating

8–10 minutes

FUNKY FAST KABOBS

Kabobs make a wicked snack at any time, but they're particularly good in the summer when they can be cooked on a barbecue. These instructions are for cooking under the broiler, but the kabobs will taste just as yummy!

Equipment

- measuring spoons
- mixing bowl
- lemon squeezer
- garlic crusher
- sharp knife
- chopping board
- slotted spoon
- plate
- plastic wrap and foil
- 8 wooden skewers
- pastry brush
- cooking tongs

What you need:

Marinade

4 tbsp olive oil

juice of 1 lemon

1 clove of garlic, crushed

salt and freshly ground black pepper

Kabobs

1 lb boned leg of lamb

2 red onions

8 mushrooms

8 cherry tomatoes

8 bay leaves

For a change!

Shrimp and cubes of salmon can be used to make tasty fish kabobs.

To make veggie kabobs, use onions, squares of red and yellow pepper, chunks of zucchini and eggplant, boiled new potatoes, and whole small tomatoes. Add some honey to the marinade for extra tastiness!

1. Mix together the marinade ingredients in a bowl. Cut the meat into 3/4-inch cubes.

2. Add the meat to the bowl and stir well. Cover and put in the fridge for 1–2 hours. Remove meat from the bowl onto a plate.

3. Peel the onions and cut into chunky wedges. Wash the tomatoes. Wipe the mushrooms. Soak the skewers in cold water for 30 minutes.

4. Push alternate meat cubes, onions, mushrooms, tomatoes, and bay leaves onto the skewers. (Take care not to prick your fingers.)

5. Preheat the broiler. Line the pan with foil. Place the kabobs on the broiler pan and brush with marinade.

6. Broil for 8–10 minutes. Turn the kabobs every 2 minutes to make sure they are cooked evenly. Serve with salad and rice or a jacket potato.

makes 8

20 minutes + rising

10–15 minutes

BEST-EVER BREAD!

Home-made bread rolls are a special treat. Nothing smells better than fresh bread straight from the oven. It's fun to make and delicious to eat!

For a change!

Use half white and half whole wheat flour to make brown rolls.

Equipment

- large mixing bowl
- wooden spoon
- measuring cups and spoons
- flour shaker
- chopping board
- plastic wrap
- knife
- baking sheet
- pastry brush
- cooling rack
- dish towel

What you need:

1 lb white bread flour

1 tsp salt

1 x ¼-oz envelope easy-blend yeast

1 tbsp vegetable oil

1½ cups warm water

2 tbsp flour for dusting

1 egg, beaten, for glazing

sesame or poppy seeds to decorate

Cook's tip!

To test that your bread is cooked, tap the base of each roll—you should hear a hollow sound.

Remember to cool your rolls before eating them!

1. Mix the flour, salt, and yeast in a bowl. Add the oil and water. Stir to form a soft dough.

2. Knead dough on a floured surface for 5–7 minutes until smooth and elastic. Place in the bowl and cover with plastic wrap. Leave in a warm place.

3. When the dough has doubled in size (about 1 hour) knead it again on a lightly floured surface until smooth. Divide into 8 equal pieces.

4. Shape half the dough into round rolls. Make the other half into cottage rolls with a small round shape on top. Place on a baking sheet.

5. Cover rolls with a dish towel. Leave to rise for 30 minutes, until the bread has doubled in size. Preheat oven to 425°F.

6. Glaze the rolls with egg and decorate with seeds. Sprinkle with flour for a soft roll. Bake in oven for 10–15 minutes until golden brown.

makes 12

25 minutes

15–20 minutes

Equipment

- mixing bowl
- measuring cups and spoons
- sifter
- fork
- round-bladed knife
- flour shaker
- rolling pin
- 3-inch cookie cutter
- tartlet pan
- measuring jug
- small skillet
- wooden spatula
- cooling rack

TASTY TARTS

You'll have a fab time making these easy-peasy tasty tarts. Get creative with your choice of fillings—anything goes! Don't forget that you can make sweet tarts too!

What you need:

¾ cup all-purpose flour

pinch of salt

¾ stick or 6 tbsp butter (or a mixture of butter and vegetable shortening)

2–3 tbsp cold water to mix

2 slices of bacon, chopped into small pieces

2 eggs, beaten

½ cup grated Cheddar cheese

⅔ cup milk

salt and freshly ground pepper

For a change!

For a veggie option, fry some sliced leeks and place in the cases before adding the egg mixture.

Make sweet tarts using raspberry jam or lemon curd, or try open mince pies with mincemeat.

1. Preheat the oven to 400°F. Sift the flour and salt into the bowl. Add the butter and rub it into the flour. It should look like breadcrumbs.

2. Sprinkle on the water and stir the mixture with a knife to make it come together. Press the pastry into a ball—the bowl should be clean.

3. On a lightly floured surface slightly flatten the pastry with your hand. Then roll out to form a rough circle about ⅛ inch thick.

4. Cut out the pastry circles and place in the tartlet pan.

5. Fry the bacon in a skillet until crisp. Mix together the eggs, cheese, bacon, milk, and seasoning.

6. Spoon the mixture into the cases. Bake in the oven for 15 minutes. Remove from the oven. Leave to cool slightly and then place on a wire rack.

TASTY FAVORITES

You can eat these delicious goodies with your family or with friends when they come round. It's simple food—and it's easy to make for any mealtime.

From old favorites such as pancakes and pizzas to scrummy burgers and chunky fish and fries—you can cook your very own take-out foods at home. Finally, impress your friends and family with a gorgeous English trifle, everyone's favorite dessert.

STEAMY SOUP!

For a cozy meal on a cold day, soup is just fab. You can feed all your family and friends with this tasty recipe—the more, the merrier!

serves 4

15 minutes

20–25 minutes

Equipment

- chopping board
- sharp knife
- garlic crusher
- large pan plus lid
- wooden spatula
- measuring cups and spoons
- measuring jug
- hand-held blender
- warm soup bowls
- grater
- lemon squeezer

What you need:

1 onion

2 leeks

1 clove of garlic

1 lb carrots

8 oz parsnips

1 tbsp olive oil

2 tbsp butter

$3\frac{1}{2}$ cups vegetable stock

grated rind and juice of 2 oranges

salt and freshly ground black pepper

1 tbsp chopped fresh parsley

For a change!

If you like a chunky soup do not blend the cooked mixture.

Make green soup by using 12 oz spinach instead of the carrots and parsnips. Flavor with nutmeg and finish off by swirling in some cream.

For a tasty topping, sprinkle on some grated cheese before serving.

1. Peel the onion and leeks and chop finely. Peel the garlic and crush. Peel the carrots and parsnips and chop into cubes.

2. Heat the oil and butter in the pan over medium heat. Add the onion and garlic and fry gently for 2–3 minutes.

3. Add the remaining vegetables and continue to cook for a further 2 minutes.

4. Pour in the stock. Cover with a tightly fitting lid and simmer over low heat for 15–20 minutes.

5. Remove the pan from the heat. Blend the soup until smooth.

6. Add the orange juice. Taste and season well. Serve the soup in warm bowls. Garnish with the orange rind and some chopped parsley.

SUPER SAVORY RICE

When you're in a big rush, rice is a great way to beat the clock and fill your tum! This recipe is for a whole meal to be served in one dish.

serves 4

10–15 minutes

14–15 minutes

Equipment

- large pan with lid
- wooden spatula
- measuring jug
- measuring cups and spoons
- skillet
- sharp knife
- chopping board
- fork
- large ovenproof serving dish

What you need:

1 heaping cup long grain rice

2½ cups vegetable or chicken stock

1 tbsp olive oil

4 strips bacon, cut into small pieces

1 small onion, finely chopped

1 red bell pepper, seeded and diced

3 oz / 1 cup button mushrooms, sliced

¾ cup frozen peas, defrosted

½ cup frozen corn, defrosted

1 tbsp chopped fresh parsley

For a change!

For a vegetarian option, leave out the bacon and serve with some grated cheese.

For a more substantial meal add 8 oz (2 cups) chopped cooked chicken to the rice.

Make yellow rice by adding ¼ tsp turmeric to the stock. Add 2 chopped scallions for extra taste.

1. Place the rice in the pan and add the stock. Bring to boil and stir. Cover and cook over low heat for 11–12 minutes.

2. While the rice is cooking, heat the oil in the skillet. Fry the bacon and onion until the bacon is cooked and the onion soft.

3. Add the red pepper and mushrooms and continue to cook for 2–3 minutes.

4. Add the peas and corn and heat through.

5. When the rice is cooked (check the pack instructions), remove pan from the heat. Gently fork through the rice to separate the grains.

6. Turn the rice into a heated serving dish and add the contents of the skillet. Mix together gently. Sprinkle with the parsley.

serves 4

20–25 minutes

20–25 minutes

PERFECT PASTA

For a delicious dinner, pasta is the ultimate yummy food. A pasta bake is a brilliant way to make large amounts of food to feed all your friends. They'll love the gorgeous sauce and crunchy topping!

What you need:

9 oz pasta shapes

¼ tsp salt

½ stick or ¼ cup butter

5 tbsp all-purpose flour

1¾ cups milk

1 cup Cheddar cheese, grated

4½ oz cooked ham, roughly chopped

4 cherry tomatoes, cut into quarters

salt and freshly ground black pepper

¼ cup Parmesan cheese, freshly grated

Equipment

- large pan
- medium pan
- measuring cups and spoons
- measuring jug
- wooden spatula
- grater
- colander
- ovenproof dish
- baking sheet

For a change!

Instead of the chopped ham and tomatoes, add 1 cup corn and 8 oz canned tuna, drained and flaked, to the pasta.

1. Preheat the oven to 400°F. Heat some water in the large pan. Add salt and bring to boil.

2. Add the pasta carefully, taking care not to splash. Cook the pasta according to the packet instructions.

3. Gently melt the butter in a pan over low heat. Add the flour and mix well. Cook mixture for 1 minute and then remove from heat.

4. Stir in the milk, a little at a time, to make a smooth sauce. Put pan back on heat. Stir while the sauce thickens so it doesn't go lumpy.

5. When the sauce boils, turn down heat and cook, stirring, for 1–2 minutes. Remove from heat. Mix in the Cheddar, ham, and tomatoes. Season.

6. Drain the pasta. Mix with the sauce. Place in ovenproof dish and sprinkle with Parmesan. Bake in oven, on a baking sheet, for 20–25 minutes.

makes 4–6

15 minutes +
10 minutes for chilling

10–12 minutes

Equipment

- mixing bowl
- fork
- measuring spoons
- chopping board
- sharp knife
- broiler pan
- foil
- pastry brush
- cooking tongs

BRILLIANT BURGERS

You can have a fab time making these tasty burgers using both meat and vegetables. Make them even more yummy by adding your favorite sauce!

What you need:

1 lb ground beef

1 onion, finely chopped

1 egg, beaten

salt and freshly ground black pepper

1 tbsp all-purpose flour for shaping

1 tbsp olive oil

To Serve

4-6 burger buns

half a lettuce

2 tomatoes

mustard, mayonnaise, tomato ketchup

For a change!

To make veggie burgers, you will need:
2 x 14 oz cans of cannellini beans, drained and rinsed
2 tbsp chopped parsley or cilantro grated rind of 1 lemon
1 beaten egg

Mix together in a blender. Season well and shape the mixture into 4 even-sized burgers. Chill for 1–2 hours and then fry in a nonstick skillet for 5 minutes on each side. Serve with salad.

1. Put the ground beef in the mixing bowl and add the onion, egg, and seasoning. Mix well.

2. Lightly flour your hands and the chopping board. Divide the mixture into 4–6 equal portions and shape into burgers.

3. Chill the burgers in the fridge for 10 minutes. Preheat the broiler. Place the chilled burgers on the broiler pan and brush with oil.

4. Broil the burgers for 4–6 minutes. Turn the burgers over, brush again with oil. Broil for a further 4–6 minutes until done.

5. Cut the buns in half. Toast them under the hot broiler if you wish. Slice the tomatoes thinly. Wash and shred the lettuce.

6. Place a handful of lettuce in each bun, then add the burger and a slice of tomato. Serve with your own choice of sauce.

makes 2 (serves 4)

15 minutes
plus rising

15–20 minutes

Equipment

- large mixing bowl
- wooden spoon
- measuring cups and spoons
- flour shaker
- chopping board
- rolling pin
- plastic wrap
- 2 baking sheets
- knife
- sifter
- bowl

PIZZA TO GO-GO!

In a lazy mood but feeling hungry? Then pizza is a great idea for a fun, easy meal. Making your own pizzas is loads of floury fun—and if you make these mini ones everyone can choose their own tasty topping.

What you need:

Base

1 ¾ cups white bread flour

½ tsp salt

2 tsp easy-blend yeast

1 tbsp vegetable oil

¾ cup warm water

2 tbsp flour for dusting

Topping

14 oz canned chopped tomatoes

2 tbsp tomato paste

2 tsp dried oregano

salt and freshly ground black pepper

2 slices of ham, torn into bite-sized pieces

5 oz mozzarella, torn into bite-sized pieces

1 yellow bell pepper, sliced

4 button mushrooms, sliced

2 tbsp olive oil

1. Make the dough following the instructions for bread on page 22, up to the end of step 3.

2. Flour your hands and the work surface. Knead the dough until smooth. Stretch into shape and roll thinly into two circles, 6 inches across.

3. Pinch up the edges of the dough. Grease the baking sheets. Place the bases on the sheets. Leave them to rise while you make the topping.

4. Preheat the oven to 425°F. Drain the tomatoes and put into a bowl with the paste and oregano. Mix and season.

5. Spread half the mixture over each base. Arrange the ham, cheese, pepper, and mushrooms on top. Brush over the olive oil.

6. Bake in the oven for 15–20 minutes until the crusts are pale golden and firm. Remove from the oven and serve.

serves 2

25 minutes

40–50 minutes

Equipment

- cook's knife
- chopping board
- measuring cups and spoons
- plate
- bowl
- fork
- shallow dish
- plastic bag
- 2 baking sheets
- pastry brush
- cooking tongs
- fish slice

CHUNKY FISH AND FRIES

Wow! With this funky recipe you can make your very own take-out food at home. The fish is coated with breadcrumbs, giving it the crunchiest, crumbliest coating!

What you need:

2 fillets of plaice or other white fish, skinned and cut into 1/2 inch wide strips

salt and pepper

2 tbsp all-purpose flour

1 egg

2 cups white or whole wheat breadcrumbs

1 tbsp finely chopped fresh parsley

2 large potatoes, scrubbed

6 tbsp olive oil

To Serve

half a lemon, cut into segments

tomato ketchup or mayonnaise

1. Preheat the oven to 400°F. Season the flour and put on a plate. Roll the strips of fish in the flour until covered.

2. Beat the egg in a bowl and pour it into a shallow dish. Dip the fish into the beaten egg. Mix the parsley and breadcrumbs. Season.

3. Put the mixture into a plastic bag. Add the fish and toss to coat thoroughly. Chill on a baking sheet in the fridge for 30 minutes.

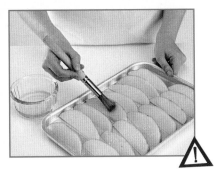  

4. Cut each potato into 8 wedges. Place on a baking sheet and brush over half the oil. Turn the potatoes to brush the other side. Season.

5. Bake the fries for 35–40 minutes until golden, turning occasionally. After 20 minutes remove the fish from fridge. Drizzle with the rest of the oil.

6. Bake at the top of the oven for 15–20 minutes, turning halfway through. Serve with the lemon and your favorite sauce.

makes 10

5 minutes

15–20 minutes

YUMMY SCRUMMY PANCAKES

Why wait for Pancake Day? These tasty treats can be mixed up in moments at any time. You can add anything you like as a topping—from sugar, maple syrup, or honey with lemon juice to lashings of chocolate sauce!

Equipment

- sifter
- mixing bowl
- wooden spoon
- measuring jug
- measuring cups and spoons
- 7-inch nonstick skillet
- wooden spatula
- baking parchment

What you need:

7/8 cup all-purpose flour

pinch of salt

1 egg, beaten

1 1/4 cups milk

10 tsp butter or oil

To Serve

lemon juice

superfine sugar

For a change!

Serve your pancakes with warmed honey or jelly. Or try them with sliced bananas and runny chocolate sauce.

Go savory and layer up the pancakes with meat or vegetable fillings. Serve with a topping of melted grated cheese.

1. Sift the flour and salt into the bowl. Make a "well" in the center; add the egg and half the milk. Beat the egg and milk together.

2. Gradually mix in the flour. When the mixture is smooth with no lumps, beat in the rest of the milk. Carefully pour the mixture into the jug.

3. Heat the pan over medium heat. Add a teaspoon of the butter or oil and swirl it around to cover the whole surface.

4. Pour in enough batter to cover the base. Swirl around the pan while tilting it so you have a thin, even layer. Cook for about 30 seconds.

5. Lift up the edge of the pancake to see if it is brown. Loosen round the edges and flip with the spatula. Cook the other side until golden brown.

6. Turn out each pancake onto a warm plate. Stack in layers with baking parchment. Cover with foil and keep warm.

Serve them hot!
Serve the pancakes while they're still hot. Sprinkle with the lemon juice and sugar and roll them up.

makes 6

30–40 minutes

1–2 hours

TASTY ENGLISH TRIFLE ★★★

With lashings of yummy custard and cream, English trifle is a wicked treat for special days. You can add almost anything you like for a tasty topping sensation—m'mmmmmm!

Equipment

- chopping board
- sharp knife
- 6 glass bowls
- measuring cups and spoons
- measuring jug
- wooden spoon
- pan
- plastic wrap
- mixing bowl
- balloon whisk

what you need:

1 jelly roll

$^{1}/_{2}$ cup orange juice (or juice from a can of fruit)

2 oz macaroons or ratafias

12 oz fresh strawberries or other fruit (fresh or canned)

Custard

5 egg yolks

3 tbsp superfine sugar

$^{1}/_{2}$ tsp vanilla extract

1 $^{3}/_{4}$ cups light cream

Topping

1 $^{1}/_{4}$ cups whipping cream

chocolate flakes to decorate

1. Cut the jelly roll into slices. Place in the bowls and pour over the fruit juice.

2. Add the macaroons to the bowls and spoon the fruit on top. Cream together the egg yolks, sugar, and vanilla extract in the jug.

3. Heat the light cream in a pan until just before boiling point. Pour the hot cream into the jug, stirring all the time until mixed.

4. Put the mixture back into the pan. Heat gently, stirring constantly, until the sauce has thickened enough to coat the back of a spoon.

5. Put the base of the pan in cold water and stir until cool. Spoon the custard over the trifle. Cover with plastic wrap and leave for 1–2 hours.

6. Just before serving, whip the cream until it is thick but soft. Spoon over the custard. Decorate and serve chilled.

WICKED TREATS

Are you ready to spoil yourself with some really delicious treats? Well, here they are! Try making chocolate crispies, probably the first "cakes" you ever make, as well as flapjacks, chocolate brownies, frosted cupcakes, cookies, and lots more.

Peppermint creams dipped in smooth dark chocolate make a brilliant gift for moms or dads. And for the ultimate luxury try the home-made ice cream—it's scrummy. So get stuck in and enjoy being just a little bit wicked!

makes 12

20 minutes

1 hour for chilling

CHOCOLATE CRISPIES ⭐

This is an easy-peasy recipe—probably one of the very first recipes you'll make. These scrunchy, chewy little cakes are delicious at any time — and they need almost no cooking.

Equipment

- mixing bowl
- large pan
- measuring cups and spoons
- wooden spoon
- knife
- tartlet pan
- 12 paper liners

What you need:

½ stick or ¼ cup butter

4 tbsp corn syrup

3½ oz milk chocolate, broken into pieces

1½ cups cornflakes

FOR A CHANGE!

You can use puffed wheat or rice crispies instead of the cornflakes.

You could use dark chocolate or even white if you like. Add ½ cup raisins to make even chewier crispie cakes.

1. Put the butter, syrup, and chocolate in the mixing bowl. Place the bowl over a large pan of simmering water.

2. Allow the butter, syrup, and chocolate to melt, stirring to mix well.

3. Remove the pan from the heat. Take the bowl out of the pan.

4. Add the cornflakes to the mixture and stir well, using a wooden spoon.

5. Carefully spoon the mixture into the paper liners. Take care you don't make them too messy.

6. Leave your crispies to set in the fridge for 1 hour. You can store them in an airtight container so they stay crisp.

makes 24

30 minutes

1 hour for chilling

Equipment

- mixing bowl
- measuring cups and spoons
- balloon whisk
- sifter
- wooden spoon
- chopping board
- teaspoon
- baking sheet lined with nonstick parchment
- fork
- small pan
- heatproof bowl

ZINGY PEPPERMINTS ★

These scrummy peppermint creams make great presents for moms, dads, grandparents—even best friends. They are easy to make, and you'll have fun dipping them in the chocolate. Don't eat all the sweets while making them!

what you need:

1 egg white

3 cups confectioners' sugar + extra for shaping

3 drops peppermint essence

2 drops green food coloring

4 oz bittersweet chocolate, broken into pieces

GIFT WRAPPED!

Arrange your peppermint creams in a prettily decorated box lined with colored tissue paper. Your granny or teacher will love them!

1. Whisk the egg white until frothy. Sift in the confectioners' sugar and mix well. Add the peppermint essence and the coloring and mix well.

2. Sprinkle some sugar onto your hands. Roll teaspoon-sized amounts of the mixture into small balls and place on the baking sheet.

3. Flatten each ball with a fork to form flat discs. Place in the fridge for 1 hour until firm.

4. Put the chocolate pieces into the heatproof bowl. Place the bowl on a pan of simmering water (about 2 inches deep).

5. When the chocolate has melted, remove from the heat and stir until smooth. Allow to cool a little.

6. Dip each candy into the chocolate until half covered. Place candies on the nonstick parchment to set. Keep in the fridge until needed.

makes 4

15–20 minutes

2 hours for chilling

MEGA CHOCOLATE MOUSSE ★ ★

This mousse is lots of fun to make—and it's totally delicious! You can learn how to melt chocolate and whisk egg whites while making a really groovy pud at the same time!

Equipment

- heatproof bowl
- pan
- tablespoon
- mixing bowl
- saucer
- eggcup
- small bowl
- teaspoon
- electric hand mixer or balloon whisk
- flexible spatula
- grater
- 4 small serving dishes

what you need:

4½ oz dark chocolate, broken into pieces

4 large eggs

2 oz white chocolate

For a change!

For a zingy "chocolate orange" flavor, add grated orange rind to the melted chocolate.

For a crunchy surprise, put some chopped nuts in the bottom of the serving dishes before adding the mousse.

1. Put the chocolate in the heatproof bowl. Place the bowl on a pan of simmering water (2 inches deep) and allow the chocolate to melt.

2. Separate the eggs following the method described on page 7. Pour the egg whites into the mixing bowl and put the yolks in the small bowl.

3. Remove the melted chocolate from the heat and stir well. Cool a little. Beat the yolks and slowly add them to the chocolate, stirring well.

50

4. Whisk the egg whites in the mixing bowl until they are white and firm and will stand up in soft peaks.

5. With the spatula, gently fold the whites into the chocolate and egg yolk mixture until evenly mixed.

6. Carefully pour the mousse into the serving dishes and leave to set in the fridge for 2 hours. Decorate with grated white chocolate.

makes about 18

10–15 minutes

25–30 minutes

SNACK-TIME FLAPJACKS

Flapjacks are a really scrummy treat for when you have the munchies! They taste great and, as they are made from oats, they're good for you too!

Equipment

- rectangular cake pan 8 x 12 inches, greased and lined with baking parchment
- large pan
- measuring cups and spoons
- wooden spoon
- flexible spatula
- round-bladed knife
- cooling rack
- airtight container for storage

What you need:

1 1/2 sticks or 3/4 cup butter

1/2 cup soft light-brown sugar

2 1/2 tbsp corn syrup

3 cups rolled oats

For a change!

You can add 1/2 cup raisins to make fruity flapjacks. For an extra-healthy option, add 1/3 cup chopped dates and 1/2 cup sunflower seeds. Try using honey instead of syrup.

For a fab treat, melt 2 oz dark chocolate and dip the flapjacks in to coat the top. Cool on a wire rack while the chocolate sets.

1. Preheat the oven to 350°F. Put the butter, sugar, and syrup into the pan.

2. Heat pan over low heat for 2–3 minutes, stirring until melted. Remove the pan from the hob, add the rolled oats, and mix.

3. Pour the mixture into the prepared cake pan. Press down well using a spatula.

4. Bake in the center of the oven for 25–30 minutes until golden but still slightly soft. Remove from the oven and leave to cool for 10 minutes.

5. Cut into squares and allow to cool completely in the pan.

6. Carefully remove the flapjacks from the pan using a knife. Store in an airtight container for up to 1 week.

COOL COOKIES ★★

These bite-sized delights are great snacks.
The only problem is that everyone will love them,
so don't be surprised if they all get eaten
very quickly!

makes 18

15 minutes

15–20 minutes

Equipment

- mixing bowl
- wooden spoon or electric hand mixer
- measuring cups and spoons
- small bowl
- fork
- sifter
- flexible spatula
- 2 baking sheets lined with baking parchment
- round-bladed knife
- cooling rack
- airtight container for storage

What you need:

1 stick + 1 tbsp butter

1/2 cup golden superfine sugar

1 large egg, beaten

1 ripe banana, mashed

1 1/3 cups self-rising flour

1 tsp mixed spice

2 tbsp milk

3/4 cup chopped mixed nuts

1/2 cup raisins

For a change!

You can replace the nuts with 1/2 cup of chocolate chips—m'mmm!

Make some dreamy peanut butter cookies by adding 2 tablespoons of peanut butter instead of the banana. Use chopped peanuts instead of the mixed nuts. Leave out the spice and raisins.

1. Preheat the oven to 375°F. Cream together the butter and sugar with a wooden spoon or mixer until light and fluffy.

2. Add the egg gradually to the mixture, beating well each time. Mash the banana and add it in, beating until the mixture is smooth.

3. Sift in the flour and spice. Fold in using a spatula. Add the milk to give a soft consistency. Fold in the nuts and fruit.

4. Drop two teaspoons per cookie of the mixture onto the lined baking sheets. Space cookies well apart (about 9 on each sheet).

5. Bake in the center of the oven for 15–20 minutes until lightly golden.

6. Remove from the oven and leave to firm up slightly. Transfer to a cooling rack using a round-bladed knife. Allow to cool before storing.

makes 8–12

20 minutes

25 minutes

GOOEY CHOCOLATE BROWNIES ★★

Brownies are the best! They're soft and gooey on the inside, and crisp on the outside—delicious! For extra crunch value you could add some chopped nuts.

Equipment

- 8-inch square cake pan
- non-stick baking parchment
- scissors
- heatproof bowl
- pan
- wooden spoon
- measuring cups and spoons
- small bowl
- fork
- sifter
- flexible spatula
- knife

What you need:

6 oz dark chocolate, broken into pieces

1 1/2 sticks or 3/4 cup butter

1 1/4 cups golden superfine sugar

pinch of salt

3 large eggs

1 scant cup all-purpose flour

2 tsp vanilla extract

1/2 cup chocolate chips

For a change!

You can use white chocolate chips or chopped walnuts as an alternative.

You can serve your brownie squares as party cakes with an individual candle on each brownie.

1. Preheat the oven to 350°F. Grease the cake pan and line it with nonstick baking parchment.

2. Place the chocolate and butter in a bowl. Melt over a pan of simmering water. Stir until smooth. Remove pan from the heat. Cool slightly.

3. Add the sugar and salt to the melted chocolate. Beat the eggs in a bowl and add them gradually to the mixture.

4. Sift the flour into the mixture and beat until smooth. Add the vanilla extract and stir in the chocolate chips.

5. Scrape the mixture into the pan. Bake for 20–25 minutes until the top is pale brown and the middle is soft. Remove from the oven.

6. Allow the brownies to cool in the pan before cutting into pieces. Remove from the pan and serve with ice cream to make a delicious dessert.

makes 12

20 minutes

15–20 minutes

Equipment

- mixing bowl
- wooden spoon
- sifter
- measuring cups and spoons
- tablespoon
- tartlet pan
- 12 paper liners
- cooling rack
- small bowl
- lemon squeezer

CRAZY CUPCAKES ★★★

With their soft sponge middles and yummy frosting topping, cupcakes are an all-time favorite treat. You can make them any color and decorate them in a funky way!

What you need:

Cupcakes

1 stick + 1 tbsp butter (softened at room temperature)

½ cup superfine sugar

2 eggs, beaten

1 cup self-rising flour

2 tbsp milk

Frosting

2 cups confectioners' sugar

1 tbsp lemon juice

1 tbsp warm water

To Decorate
candies, chocolate buttons, sprinklers, silver balls, grated coconut, and glacé cherries

For a change!
You can make some funky frosting colors for your cupcakes. Divide the mixture into small bowls and add a few drops of different coloring to each one.

1. Preheat the oven to 375°F. Use a wooden spoon to cream the butter and sugar until light and fluffy.

2. Add the eggs a little at a time, beating well after each addition. Sift the flour into the bowl and carefully fold in using a tablespoon.

3. Mix in the milk. Stir until the mixture is smooth and drops off the spoon easily. Divide the mixture between the paper liners (in the pan).

4. Bake in the oven for 15–20 minutes until the cakes are risen and golden brown. Remove from the oven and put on a cooling rack.

5. Sift the confectioners' sugar into the bowl. Add the lemon juice and stir in the warm water. Mix until thick and smooth.

6. Spoon the frosting onto the cakes. Spread to the liner edges with the back of a teaspoon. Use your imagination to decorate!

each recipe
serves 6

15 minutes
+ cooling

3–4 hours for
freezing

DREAMY ICE CREAM

You can make loads of these dreamy ice-cream mixtures without even needing a special ice-cream maker. Just follow these simple recipes and get scooping!

Equipment

- small pan
- wooden spoon
- measuring cups and spoons
- mixing bowl
- balloon whisk
- flexible spatula
- 2 x 1-quart plastic freezer boxes with lids
- fork

What you need:

Toffee Ice Cream

3¾ tbsp corn syrup

½ cup light soft-brown sugar

½ stick or ¼ cup butter

1 tsp vanilla extract

⅔ cup heavy cream

2 full cups thick, creamy yogurt

3½ oz fudge, chopped into small pieces

Berry Ice Cream

150 ml fruit pureé, made from frozen pack of forest fruits or red berries, thawed

14 oz or 1¾ cups vanilla-flavored yogurt

14 oz fromage frais

TOFFEE ICE CREAM

1. Place the syrup, sugar, and butter in a pan over a low heat. Stir to dissolve the sugar and melt the butter. Take off the heat. Stir in the vanilla.

2. Beat the cream until soft and thick. Fold in the yogurt, cooled toffee sauce, and fudge. Pour the mixture into the box. Cover and freeze for 1 hour.

3. Stir the frozen mixture and return to the freezer for 1 hour. Repeat until the mixture is frozen. Place in the fridge for 30 minutes before serving.

BERRY ICE CREAM

1. Mash the thawed fruits with a fork until they form a purée.

2. Pour the yogurt and the fromage frais into a mixing bowl. Carefully stir in the fruit purée using a spatula.

3. Pour the mixture into a plastic box. Cover and freeze for 1 hour. Follow the instructions in step 3 on the opposite page.

For a change!

Instead of the frozen forest fruits, you could use fresh raspberries or strawberries when in season.

COOKING THINGS

1 electric blender
2 scale
3 food processor
4 grater
5 tongs
6 electric hand mixer

7 beaters
8 freezer box
9 electric hand blender
10 balloon whisk

1 pans
2 colander
3 cake pan
4 bun pan
5 baking sheet
6 mixing bowl

7 sifter
8 measuring jug
9 lemon squeezer
10 rolling pin
11 oven mitts
12 cooling rack

1 measuring cups
2 pastry brush
3 flour shaker
4 plastic spatula
5 slotted spoon
6 fish slice
7 scissors
8 sharp knives

9 chopping board
10 garlic crusher
11 cookie cutter
12 vegetable peeler
13 wooden skewers
14 wooden spoon
15 wooden spatula

COOKING WORDS

beat
To mix ingredients together, using a wooden spoon or hand mixer, until soft and stretchy.

blend
To mix together, using a blender or food processor, to make a liquid or a smooth mix.

chop
To chop food into small pieces with a knife.

cream
To beat butter and sugar together using a wooden spoon or hand mixer; the creamed mixture should be smooth and pale.

drain
To pour off water from cooked foods, using a strainer or a colander.

drizzle
To pour a trickle over the top of food.

fold in
To mix gently; use a metal spoon or spatula so that you don't remove the air beaten in earlier.

garnish
To decorate a savory dish with whole or chopped herbs, chopped nuts, sliced tomatoes, and so on.

glaze
To brush dough with egg yolk or milk so that it looks shiny and golden when baked.

grease
To brush a baking sheet or cake pan with oil or rub with butter to stop the food from sticking.

knead
To work with bread dough on a board so that it becomes smooth and elastic.

rise
To put bread dough in a warm place so the yeast can work. The dough should double in size.

rub in
To rub butter into flour, using the tips of your fingers, to produce a mixture that looks like breadcrumbs.

season
To add salt and pepper to food to increase its taste.

sift
To use a sifter to remove any lumps from sugar or flour before adding them to a mixture; sifting also adds air to the mix.

simmer
To cook a liquid in a pan so that it bubbles gently but does not boil.

whisk
To beat a mixture very hard to add air so that the mixture becomes thick. Use either a balloon whisk or an electric hand mixer.

INDEx